MY
CHRISTMAS
BIBLE

www.CTAinc.com

Scripture quotations are from The Holy Bible, King James Version.

Copyright © 2004 by CTA, Inc.,
1625 Larkin Williams Rd., Fenton, MO 63026-1205.

ISBN 0-9747923-3-0
Printed in Thailand

God's Promise to Send Jesus to Be Our Savior

Behold, a virgin shall conceive, and bear a son, and shall call his name Immanuel.

Isaiah 7:14

(Immanuel means "God is with us.")

★For unto us a child is born,
unto us a son is given:
and the government shall be
upon his shoulder: and his
name shall be called
   Wonderful, Counsellor,
   The mighty God,
   The everlasting Father,
   The Prince of Peace.

Isaiah 9:6

But thou, Bethlehem Ephratah, though thou be little among the thousands of Judah, yet out of thee shall he come forth unto me that is to be ruler in Israel.

Micah 5:2

Baby Jesus
Is Born!

And it came to pass in those days, that there went out a decree from Caesar Augustus that all the world should be taxed. . . . And all went to be taxed, every one into his own city.

Luke 2:1–3

And Joseph also went up from Galilee, out of the city of Nazareth, into Judaea, unto the city of David, which is called Bethlehem; (because he was of the house and lineage of David:) To be taxed with Mary his espoused wife, being great with child.

Luke 2:4–5

And so it was, that, while they were there, the days were accomplished that she should be delivered.

And she brought forth her firstborn son, and wrapped him in swaddling clothes, and laid him in a manger; because there was no room for them in the inn.

Luke 2:6–7

Angels,
Shepherds,
and
Wise Men

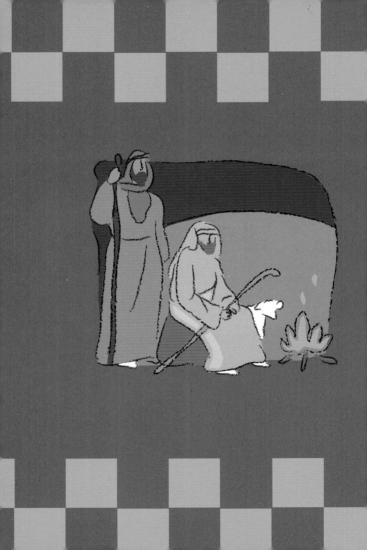

And there were in the same country shepherds abiding in the field, keeping watch over their flock by night.

Luke 2:8

And, lo, the angel of the Lord
came upon them, and the glory of
the Lord shone round about them:
and they were sore afraid.

And the angel said unto them, Fear
not: for, behold, I bring you good
tidings of great joy, which shall be
to all people. For unto you is born
this day in the city of David a
Saviour, which is Christ the Lord.

Luke 2:9–11

And this shall be a sign unto you;
Ye shall find the babe wrapped
in swaddling clothes, lying in a
manger.

And suddenly there was with the
angel a multitude of the heavenly
host praising God, and saying,
Glory to God in the highest,
and on earth peace, good will
toward men.

Luke 2:12–14

And it came to pass, as the
angels were gone away from them
into heaven, the shepherds said
one to another,
Let us now go even unto
Bethlehem, and see this thing
which is come to pass, which the
Lord hath made known unto us.

Luke 2:15

Now when Jesus was born in Bethlehem of Judaea in the days of Herod the king, behold, there came wise men from the east to Jerusalem,

Saying, Where is he that is born King of the Jews? for we have seen his star in the east, and are come to worship him.

Matthew 2:1–2

And when they were come into the house, they saw the young child with Mary his mother, and fell down, and worshipped him: and when they had opened their treasures, they presented unto him gifts; gold, and frankincense, and myrrh.

Matthew 2:11

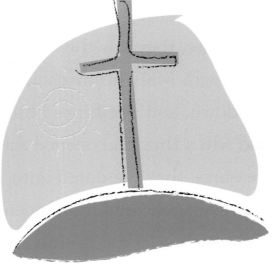

Jesus,
My Savior!

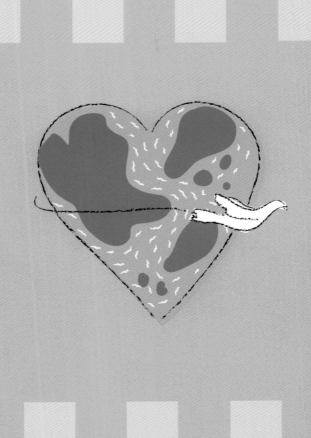

*For God so loved the world, that he gave his only begotten Son, that whosoever believeth in him should not perish, but have everlasting life.

John 3:16

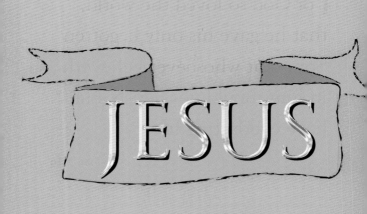

[The angel said to Joseph,]
Thou shalt call his name
JESUS: for he shall save his
people from their sins.

Matthew 1:21

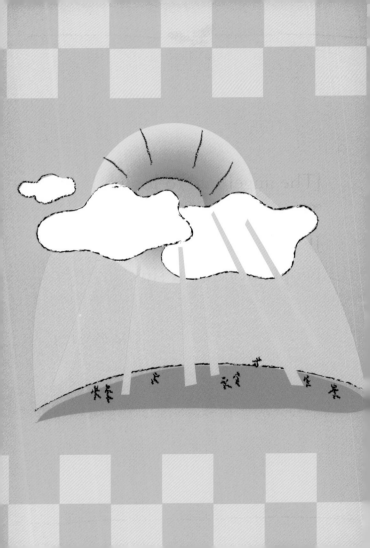

Behold, what manner of love
the Father hath bestowed upon us,
that we should be called the sons
of God. . . .

Beloved, now are we the sons of
God, and it doth not yet appear
what we shall be: but we know
that, when he shall appear, we
shall be like him; for we shall see
him as he is.

1 John 3:1–2